NEW CRAFTS

MOSAICS

NEW CRAFTS

MOSAICS

**25 exciting projects to create, using
glass, tiles and marble**

HELEN BAIRD

Photography by Tim Imrie

LORENZ BOOKS

This edition is published by Lorenz Books,
an imprint of Anness Publishing Ltd,
Blaby Road,
Wigston,
Leicestershire
LE18 4SE

info@anness.com

www.lorenzbooks.com; www.annesspublishing.com

If you like the images in this book and would
like to investigate using them for publishing,
promotions or advertising, please visit our website
www.practicalpictures.com for more information.

© Anness Publishing Ltd 2013

Publisher: Joanna Lorenz
Editors: Lindsay Porter and Anne Hildyard
Designer: Lilian Lindblom
Photographer: Tim Imrie
Stylist: Fanny Ward
Illustrators: Madeleine David and
    Vana Haggerty
Production Controller: Mai-Ling Collyer

DISCLAIMER
Learning a new craft is great fun and can fill many rewarding hours, but
some tools may need to be handled with care. The author and publishers
have made every effort to ensure that all instructions in this book are
accurate and safe, and therefore cannot accept liability for any resulting
injury, damage or loss to persons or property, however it may arise.

PUBLISHER'S NOTE
Although the advice and information in this book are believed to be
accurate and true at the time of going to press, neither the authors nor
the publisher can accept any legal responsibility or liability for any errors
or omissions that may have been made nor for any inaccuracies nor for
any loss, harm or injury that comes about from following instructions or
advice in this book.

Bracketed terms are intended for American readers.

PICTURE CREDITS
Thanks to e.t. archive for the photographs on
pages 8, 9, 10 and 11.

CONTENTS

INTRODUCTION

To embark upon making a mosaic may seem like a daunting task, but with some instruction and a little patience, it is remarkably easy. Mosaics don't have to look absolutely perfect, since part of their charm is their individuality. And, they can be made out of any material that can be embedded into or stuck on to another.

Traditional materials such as smalti, vitreous glass and stone are still used, but modern artists also make mosaics from tiles, crockery, mirror and glass, which can be broken into regular pieces or smashed up haphazardly for a crazy paving effect. Interesting designs can also be made from materials such as beads, shells, stones, seeds, and fragments of plastic, metal and wood. Before beginning to experiment, it is useful to find out about the techniques involved, and understand the properties of the various materials. Whether you choose to make a classic Roman urn or a more prosaic splashback for the bathroom, you will gain huge satisfaction from experimenting with this versatile and fascinating art.

Left: Almost any surface can be embellished with mosaics, from simple ceramic tiles to glass or wood – or even plastic.

HISTORY OF MOSAICS

The word 'mosaic' conjures up images of Roman floor and wall designs, pictures made up of small geometric-shaped stones. This is only part of the story, however, even though the word mosaic does have its origins in Italy. As a medium, mosaic certainly existed long before the Romans and has been used in many ways and for various purposes, by subsequent cultures and civilizations until the present day. Mosaic has been defined as 'a surface decoration made by inlaying small pieces of varyingly coloured material to form a pattern or picture'. While these small pieces of material are used together to form a whole surface pattern or design, they retain their individual identities within the mosaic. Although mosaics often have a purely decorative function, because the materials used to make them are usually very hard-wearing they are often given the functional role of floor or wall covering as well.

The earliest surviving mosaics were made in about 3000BC by the Sumerians in ancient Mesopotamia, the area now known as Iraq. These consisted of arrangements of coloured clay pegs that were pressed into wall surfaces. Later the Egyptians used fragments of coloured materials and semi-precious stones to embellish walls and to inlay furniture, decorative objects and items of jewellery.

Ancient Greece is the earliest civilization known to have used natural stones and pebbles in varying colours to create permanent designs, and it was probably the originator of what we today think of as 'mosaic'. The Romans built on this technique, standardizing practices by cutting natural stone into regular cubes. They also used fired clay and a little glass for special effects. Another Roman innovation was the use of cements and mortars. These made their mosaics much more durable than those of their predecessors, and as a result there are many surviving examples of floor and wall mosaics throughout countries that were once part of the Roman Empire.

Right: A mosaic portrait of a Roman woman, dating from the 1st century AD. The colour and pattern of the mosaic pieces have been used to great effect in creating the features.

Left: Roman pavement mosaic depicting a banquet with musicians, 1st–2nd century AD.

Below: Detail from the church of San Vitale, Ravenna, 6th century AD, showing the Emperor Justinian.

The Romans used an extraordinarily varied range of styles and subjects in their mosaics – from realistic, observed studies of everyday life to naive garden mosaics, and from depictions of the gods in the received format to purely decorative designs and geometric borders.

These early mosaics were executed in the natural colours of the materials they were made from, such as greys, terracotta, ochre, black, white, muted blues and greens. The growth of Christianity introduced new subject matter, but techniques and colour remained broadly unchanged until the Byzantine era, usually dated as beginning with the reign of the Emperor Justinian in Ravenna, about AD527. This was to be a rich and innovative period in the history of mosaic, exemplified by the luminous creations adorning Byzantine churches.

At this time, Ravenna was a wealthy imperial town and the main trading link between East and West. It is here that the best examples of Byzantine mosaic can be found, and the influence of Eastern art is apparent in the designs, such as the large Egyptian eyes, flattened shapes and ordered poses. This iconoclastic style was rendered with a new kind of tesserae – glass 'smalti'. Glass, which previously had been used sparingly for highlights, now became the main component of mosaics. It was fired with metallic oxides, copper and marble or had gold and silver leaf sandwiched in it. This new material gave mosaic artists access to a large palette of luminous colours. They also developed the technique of setting the pieces into the mortar bed at varying angles, thus achieving wonderful effects with the reflective qualities of glass.

When Ravenna ceased to be the main link between Europe and Asia, and its trade and wealth were taken over by Venice, the art of mosaic-making soon followed. Records show that a school of Venetian mosaicists was established as early as AD979. The traditions of the Byzantine school were carried on there, then moved to Constantinople, the centre of orthodox Christianity at the time, and the art reached its peak in the 13th century.

With the dawning of the Renaissance, mosaicists became preoccupied with refining their technical abilities and, as with painters of the time, they tried to represent space, line and form. By the late 16th century, mosaic was imitating painting so completely that mosaicists were able to mimic brushstrokes, as, for example, in the mosaics created in St. Peter's Basilica in Rome.

Above: Interior of San Vitale, Ravenna, showing the apse and Byzantine columns.

During this period, the art of mosaic-making was superseded by fresco painting. The mosaics that did continue to be created tended to be copies of paintings. This trend persisted right up to the 20th century. As a result, the mosaicist had become a master craftworker and copyist rather than an original artist.

At the beginning of the 20th century, the Art Nouveau movement gave artists a new direction, and mosaic was seen as an artistic medium that could be celebrated for its own qualities. Pure pattern re-emerged and forms were simplified and stylized.

Mosaic was further freed with the onset of modernism. The best-known exponent of mosaic in this era was the architect Antonio Gaudí (1852–1926). He covered the large exterior surfaces of his buildings, both plain and formed, with irregularly shaped coloured tiles. He also commissioned prominent modern artists of the time, such as Kokoschka, Klimt and Chagall, to make designs for the mosaics that clad his buildings. Examples of his mosaics include the façade of Casa Battló, the spires of the Sagrada Familia, the serpentine benches on the terrace of Güell Park and at Barcelona's cathedral.

A collaborator of Gaudí, José Maria Jujal, is also interesting for the ceramic medallions he made for the ceiling of the Hypostyle Hall in Güell Park. He set brilliantly coloured mosaic pieces (tesserae) against ceramic fragments, such as bases of bottles, cups and dishes, arranged in patterns of stars and spirals.

But the history of mosaics is not confined to Western Europe. In Central America, long before the arrival of Europeans, the Aztecs and Mayas developed mosaic techniques separately from the rest of the world. There, mosaic was not used to convey images or systematic patterns, as was the tradition in Europe. Rather, it was simply used to embellish three-dimensional

forms, very beautifully, using tesserae made from fragments of precious materials, most often turquoise and coral. These objects were often of a votive or ceremonial nature, such as skulls, weapons and carved snakes, and were encrusted with a variety of precious materials to give them colour, beauty and importance.

Mosaic is an important component of Islamic art. The designs are closely related to the buildings in which they are set and seem to rise naturally from the architecture.

A fine example of the Islamic mosaic tradition can be seen in the 14th-century palace of the Alhambra in Granada, Spain, and Muslim craftsmen still construct complicated geometric mosaics today.

Many cultures use mosaic-like effects to adorn buildings and objects. In African art, for example, everyday objects are often studded with tacks or are covered in coloured beads. The effect is that of mosaic, although the method by which the pieces are attached differs.

Above: Antonio Gaudi's mosaic tiles in the garden at Belleguarde, Barcelona.

The handwoven carpets of India and Turkey are in many ways comparable to the medium of mosaic. The patterns are made up of individual units of colour and, indeed, these can be useful as ideas for designs. Today, mosaic artists draw their inspiration from many different cultures and traditions and combine these influences with techniques and ideas that developed in Europe.

GALLERY

Mosaic-making is an ancient craft with a rich history. Today, designers and craftspeople are drawn to the medium for its decorative qualities and versatility. Mosaics can be made from all manner of materials, from the traditional smalti and tesserae, to crockery, glass, mirrors and even plastic. These examples of contemporary work range from pieces that reflect their classical antecedents, to modern abstract designs.

Above: TEMPLE
Inspired by the embroidered decorations found in Rajasthan, this colourful piece incorporates vitreous glass and broken tiles.
Nikki Greaves

Above right: ADAM AND EVE
This pillar is modern in its design and materials, using a 'crazy paving' effect to create the pattern set into a solid concrete base, while the theme
depicted reflects the historical precedents of mosaic decoration.
Helen Baird

Right: STILETTOS
These eye-catching sculptures were created from pieces
of mirrored glass on sculpted polystyrene (Styrofoam) bases. The sinuous, almost organic shape of the shoes is enhanced by the reflective qualities of the mirror.
Rebecca Newnham

Left: ABSTRACT TABLE
The perfect combination of old and new, resulting in a contemporary yet pleasingly classic piece. The tonal range and carefully considered sizes of the mosaic pieces create a harmonious design.
Zoe Candlin

Below: PICTURE FRAMES
The artist has made great use of contrasting textures in these delightful picture frames, setting jewel-bright glass spheres and fragments into rough plaster backgrounds.
Luciana Izzi

Right: BEFORE SCHOOL DINNER
A wonderfully quirky piece composed of fragments of china set on a wok base.
Cleo Mussi

Right: FISH PANEL
This relatively simple design makes use of the inherent pattern-making qualities of tesserae to great effect. While the background pieces are composed in a regular grid pattern, the fish are made of fragments of tiles that suggest both scales and the movement of the fish through water.
Mosaic Workshop

Below:
EMBELLISHED CABINET
This charming cabinet is made of papier-mâché, decorated with a mosaic top. Naive designs worked in pulped paper on the sides of the cabinet echo the style of the parrot mosaic design on the top of the piece of furniture.
Emma Sprawson

Left: SUNFLOWER TABLE
Broken china and discarded crockery are used to make up this delightful table design.
Norma Vondee

Right: THE
ALLOTMENT
Whole vitreous glass
tiles are combined
with carefully shaped
pieces to make up
this charming design.
The perspective is
intentionally flattened,
creating an effect
reminiscent of early
folk-art designs.
Mosaic Workshop

Above: BIRD TABLE
Here, the mosaic pattern was inlaid into a specially built wooden table top, allowing the border of the table to become part of the design. The flowing lines and bird patterns are reminiscent of many medieval tapestry designs. Elaine Goodwin

Left: SILVER GILT MIRROR
For this elegant design, the natural beauty and cool colours of the materials are used to great effect. Estitxu Garcia

Right: FIRE SALAMANDER Traditional marble tiles were used to produce this paving slab. Movement and interest are created by the positioning of the marble tesserae in the manner of early Classical mosaicwork.
Martin Cheek

Right: GREEK TABLE Simplicity itself, this pleasing table design is reminiscent of Greek friezes.
Norma Vondee

MATERIALS

Tesserae is the term given to the individual pieces which, when put together, make a mosaic. These can be made from almost any solid substance. For practical purposes, only those most commonly used are listed in this book. The choice of tesserae depends upon the uses of the mosaic, for example, a hard-wearing material is needed for a mosaic that will be walked on. Take this into account when deciding on your materials.

Adhesives When choosing the correct adhesive, two considerations must be taken into account. First, should the glue be waterproof? Second, is the glue suitable for sticking the tesserae to the base? PVA (white) glue is most often used and is excellent for securing most tesserae to a wooden base. For sticking tesserae to glass, use silicone sealant. For sticking glass to metal, use epoxy resin glue, which should also be used with other materials when greater strength or weather resistance is required.

Bases Mosaic can be made on top of almost any surface, as long as it is rigid and correctly pre-treated and the environment in which the mosaic is to be placed is taken into account. For example, if a mosaic is being made to stand outside, it would be unwise to secure it to a base material that may warp or expand when exposed to damp conditions. One of the most popular bases for a mosaic with a flat surface, such as a table top, is plywood (exterior-grade or marine), as it is strong and warp-resistant.

Cement mortar is often used as the base for a mosaic. It can also be used to secure the mosaic to its base as well as to grout between the tesserae. It is very easy and cheap to make: three parts builder's sand mixed with one part cement and enough water to make it pliable. Cements are also available with adhesive added to them. This gives the cement extra adhesive qualities and more flexibility. Specialist dyes can also be added to cement.

Crockery Old plates and cups can make very interesting tesserae. Often they have patterns that can be incorporated into the design of the mosaic. However, the uneven surface they create makes them unsuitable for use in some mosaics.

Grout Mosaics are often grouted with cement; however, specialist grouts are also used. These usually have a smoother texture and can be bought in many colours. They can also be coloured with most water-based household and acrylic paints.

Marble comes in a wide range of colours and can be bought pre-cut into small squares. It is possible to cut marble tiles into squares yourself, but special tools are needed to do this (hammer-and-hardie). Marble tiles can also be broken up using a household hammer. When doing this, wear protective eye covering, or cover the marble with sacking (heavy cloth).

Mirror Add shards of broken mirror to add reflective qualities. Cover the mirror with sacking and break with a hammer, or use tile nippers to cut more exact shapes.

Paper This is useful as a base when creating mosaics using the semi-indirect method. (See Basic Techniques)

Plastic Although not traditional, interesting effects can be achieved using plastic or other man-made materials.

Shellac This can be used for sealing the finished pieces.

Smalti This is opaque glass cut into regular-shaped chunks. Made by firing glass with oxides, metals and powdered marble, it has a softly reflective surface

and is available in a large variety of colours. Gold and silver smalti are made by sandwiching gold and silver leaf in transparent, coloured glass.

Tiles Ceramic tiles are available in a huge range of colours and textures. Most can be cut with tile nippers, but if not, they can usually be broken with a hammer (protect your eyes when doing this).

Vitreous glass These are manufactured glass squares, flat on one side and corrugated on the other. The colour range is not quite as large as that of smalti, but they are a lot cheaper and easier to cut. Also, the material is very hard-wearing.

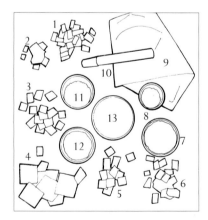

Key
1 Glass smalti
2 Broken mirror
3 Vitreous glass
4 Broken tiles
5 Gold-leaf smalti
6 Broken crockery
7 Powdered cement
8 Epoxy resin glue
9 Brown paper
10 Paper glue
11 Powdered tile grout
12 PVA (white) glue
13 Shellac

EQUIPMENT

Many of the tools needed to make mosaics are easy to find, and most can be purchased in any good hardware store. However, most households already have the necessary equipment, particularly for designing and cleaning. Before investing in specialist equipment, it is a good idea to check your cupboards. You may find many of the tools you need lurking in the back.

Abrasive paper Coarse-grade abrasive paper can be used to sand down the edges of wooden base materials. Fine-grade abrasive paper can be used in some instances for cleaning.

Bench vice or clamps This may be useful for cutting out the wooden base material.

Bradawl Use for punching holes in wooden bases if they require hanging.

Brushes If applying grout in powdered form, use a soft brush to spread the powder in the spaces between the tesserae and to remove any excess. Use a stiff-bristled brush, such as an old nailbrush, to clean dried grout off the finished mosaic. Fine artists' paintbrushes may be used to apply adhesive to small tile pieces.

Chalk Use to sketch on to the base.

Craft (utility) knife When making designs using the indirect or semi-indirect method, it may be necessary to cut the background paper away from the tesserae pieces. A sharp blade will help to do this.

Dust mask It is advisable to wear a dust mask when working with powdered grout or cement, or when cleaning with dilute hydrochloric acid.

Dilute hydrochloric acid This can be used for cleaning cement-based grout from the finished mosaic but is not strictly necessary. If using, follow proper safety procedures by protecting your eyes and hands, wearing a mask and working in a well-ventilated area if not outdoors.

Drill A good drill with hole-boring and rebating (rabbeting) bits may be useful for some projects, particularly if you want to add hanging devices.

Felt-tipped pen Draw your design on to the base material with a felt-tipped pen.

Hammer Use to smash ceramic or mirror tiles into shards. Cover with a piece of sacking (heavy cloth).

Mixing containers Old mixing bowls, buckets or even washing-up bowls are useful for mixing up grout and cement.

Palette knife (metal spatula) A palette knife or flexible kitchen knife can be used for spreading cement-based adhesive on to your base.

Pencil A pencil point or sharp stick may be used to apply glue to tiny pieces of tesserae.

Protective gloves Rubber gloves should always be used when cleaning with dilute hydrochloric acid, and may be used to apply grouting to tesserae. Heavy work gloves should be worn whenever you are breaking tesserae with a hammer.

Rulers and tape measures Use to measure and plan designs that require accuracy.

Sacking (heavy cloth) or old cloths Use to cover tiles before smashing with a hammer to prevent small pieces from dispersing.

Safety goggles Wear when breaking tiles with a hammer or when cleaning finished mosaics with dilute hydrochloric acid.

Saws Different types of saw are useful for cutting your wooden base material. Use a hacksaw for basic shapes, and a jigsaw (saber saw) for more complicated designs.

Spatula Use a spatula for spreading glue or other smooth adhesives, such as cellulose filler, on to your base material.

Sponges and old cloths Use for wiping off excess adhesive and for polishing.

Squeegee This may be used to apply grout between tesserae, particularly if the surface of the design is very flat.

Tile nippers These are invaluable for cutting tesserae to any shape required. For shapes with rounded edges use to nibble away the edges, a small amount at a time, until the desired shape is achieved.

Trowel or notched cement spreader Use either of these for spreading grout and cement-based adhesive.

Key

1 Jigsaw (saber saw)	15 Soft brush
2 Vice	16 Fine paintbrush
3 Pencil	17 Tape measure
4 Ruler	18 Grout spreader
5 Felt-tipped pen	19 Flexible knife
6 Hammer	20 Sponge
7 Right-angled ruler	21 Dust mask
8 D-clamp	22 Abrasive paper
9 Craft (utility) knife	23 Tile nippers
10 Pliers	24 Nailbrush
11 Scissors	25 Bradawl
12 Trowel	26 Safety goggles
13 Spatula	27 Plant mister
14 Drill	28 Chalk
	29 Masking tape

Basic Techniques

When embarking on your first mosaic, it is advisable to use a very simple design. Often, these uncomplicated designs can produce the most effective mosaics. Concentrate on combinations of the colours and textures in the tesserae you choose. Lay the tesserae side by side and look at the effect of the different elements. When you are sure the combinations work, you can commit yourself to sticking the tesserae to the base.

CUTTING TESSERAE

1 There are three basic methods for cutting tesserae. The first and most flexible method is to use tile nippers, which are very simple to operate. Hold the material to be cut between the tips of the cutting edges of the nippers. Squeeze the handles together, and the tesserae should break in two along the line of impact. Nippers are also useful for making a specific shape

2 When breaking up larger materials, and if regular shapes are not required, the simplest technique is to break the tesserae with a hammer. When doing this, always wear a pair of goggles or cover the tesserae with sacking (heavy cloth).

3 The third technique is to use a hammer-and-hardie. This specialist piece of equipment consists of a small tungsten-tipped anvil, which should be embedded in a log, and a curved tungsten-tipped hammer. It is used for cutting smalti or marble into regular shapes. Hold the material to be cut over the anvil between your thumb and forefinger, then bring down the hammer on the material, in line with the tip of the anvil. The smalti or marble should fracture cleanly along the line of impact.

SETTING TESSERAE ON THE BASE

Direct Method

This simple method is used for most of the projects illustrated in this book. The tesserae are simply stuck, face up, on to the base. When setting a mosaic on a three-dimensional object or an uneven surface, this method may be the only feasible way of working.

1 For the direct method, simply cover the base with a layer of cement or tile adhesive and push the tesserae into it randomly.

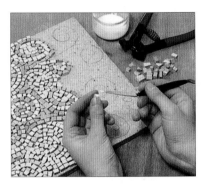

2 If you are following a more exacting design, apply cement or tile adhesive to the individual tesserae and then stick them to the base. In this way, any design drawn on the base will not be obscured by having adhesive spread all over it.

3 If the tesserae have a reflective quality, the direct method allows them to be laid on the base at different angles. This causes light to be reflected at different angles, and the mosaic will appear to shimmer.

Indirect Method

Originally this technique was devised as a way of making large-scale mosaics off-site, so that they could be transported ready made, then laid in position. When using this method, the design is sectioned into manageable areas, and each area is formed into a mosaic slab, as described below. The slabs are transported to the chosen site and fitted together to form the finished mosaic.

1 Make a wooden frame to the desired proportions of the finished slab, fixing the corners with 2.5cm (1in) screws. Grease the inside of the frame with petroleum jelly to help prevent the cement sticking to the wood. Make a template of the slab by drawing around the inside of the frame on brown paper. Draw a simple design on the paper within the marked parameters, taking care to leave a 2mm (1⁄16in) margin around the outer edge.

2 Cut vitreous glass tesserae to the required shape and size. Using a suitable water-soluble adhesive, paste them face down on to the brown paper, carefully following the lines of your design. Other tesserae can be used for this method, but vitreous glass has the advantage of being the same colour front and back, therefore greatly reducing the likelihood of making mistakes when positioning individual pieces.

3 When the glued tesserae have dried, place the frame carefully over them, using the guidelines to make sure the frame is in exactly the right position. Sprinkle dry sand over the design and use a soft brush to nudge the sand into the crevices between the tesserae.

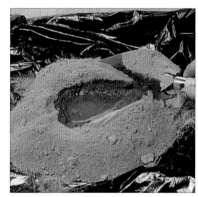

4 On a board, mix three parts builder's sand with one part cement. When this is fully mixed, pile it into a mound and make a well in the middle. Pour water into the well and mix with a trowel. Continue to add water and mix until the consistency of the resulting mortar is pliable but not runny.

5 Carefully half-fill the frame with this mortar, making sure it is pressed into the corners. Cut a square of chicken-wire a little smaller than the frame, and place this on top of the cement mortar; make sure that the wire does not touch the sides of the frame. Fill the frame with the remainder of the mortar. Smooth the surface with the trowel or a straight piece of wood. Place damp newspapers then plastic sheeting over the frame and leave for five or six days to dry. The drying has to be as slow as possible to allow the slab to dry uniformly, and to avoid the possibility of cracks forming.

6 When dry, turn over the slab and its frame and dampen the brown paper with a sponge. The paper should then peel away cleanly. Loosen the screws holding the frame together and remove the slab from the frame. To finish off, the face of the slab may need grouting and cleaning.

Semi-indirect or Half-and-half

This method is a combination of the direct and indirect methods described above. As with the fully indirect method, the tesserae are glued into position away from the intended site but are actually set into cement on site. This method allows mosaics to be made up easily in irregular shapes. Their light weight is especially good for fixing the mosaics to walls. Like the indirect method, this technique is especially useful when a smooth, flat surface is required.

1 Draw the design on brown paper and stick the tesserae face down on to it, using a water-soluble glue.

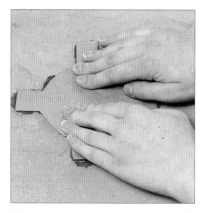

2 Spread mortar over the area designated for the mosaic. A template of the mosaic can be used to mark the proportions. Press the tesserae into the mortar, paper side up.

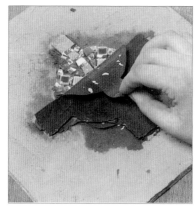

3 Leave for 24 hours to dry; if the mosaic is situated outside, prevent it from getting wet. When it is dry, dampen the paper with a wet sponge and, once the moisture has soaked through to the glue, peel away the paper, leaving the tesserae in position. The mosaic surface is now ready to be grouted and cleaned.

4 Another method of applying a mosaic in a semi-indirect fashion is to stick the tesserae in position on to netting using a PVA (white) adhesive, but with the tesserae placed face up.

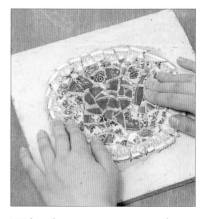

5 When the tesserae are secure on the netting, press the mosaic, face up, into cement. Leave to dry before grouting and cleaning. This semi-indirect method can result in an undulating surface like that created when working with the direct method.

GROUTING

Mosaics are grouted primarily to give them extra strength and a smoother finished surface. The process has the added bonus of tying the tesserae together and making the mosaic look complete. Often, mosaics are left ungrouted. This is usual when smalti are used, as the ungrouted surface is considered more expressive.

When choosing which grout to use, consider the mosaic's location and therefore whether it will need to be waterproof and/or hard-wearing. Grouts come ready-mixed or in powder form. Usually, they are applied to the mosaic ready-mixed. On flat surfaces, a squeegee can be used to spread the grout over the surface and push it between the crevices.

1 When grouting three-dimensional mosaics or uneven surfaces, it is easiest to first spread the grout over the surface with a flexible knife.

2 Then, wearing rubber gloves, rub the grout into the crevices.

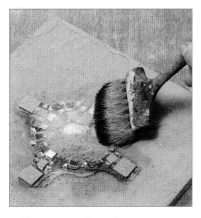

3 When grouting large, flat areas, it is useful to spread the grout while it is in powder form. Use a powdered cement-based adhesive and spoon it on to the surface, then spread it with a soft brush.

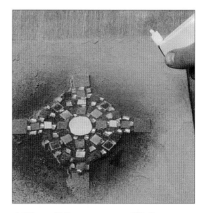

4 When all the crevices are filled, spray the mosaic with water using a household plant mister. Make sure enough water is sprayed and absorbed into the cement.

You will probably need to repeat the process, as cement shrinks when wetted.

CLEANING

It is advisable to get rid of most of the excess grout while it is still wet. Most purpose-made grouts can be scrubbed from the surface using a stiff-bristled brush, such as a nailbrush, and then polished off. Cement mortars and cement-based adhesives need rougher treatment, and you will probably need to use abrasive paper. A quicker alternative is to dilute hydrochloric acid and paint it on to the surface to dissolve the excess cement. This process should be done outside, as it gives off toxic fumes. When the excess cement has fizzed away, wash off the residue of acid from the mosaic with plenty of water.

BOTTLE

This bottle project is ideal for beginners who want to experiment with vitreous glass. The design is very loose and requires virtually no drawing ability. It relies on the effects created by the juxtaposition of colours and textures. Relatively inexpensive bags of tesserae in mixed colours can be bought from specialist mosaic suppliers, and it is worth experimenting with these before purchasing larger quantities of a single colour. Decorating a bottle like this is also a good way of using up odd bits of tesserae that have been left over from other projects.

1 Clean the bottle, rub off the label and dry thoroughly. Dab silicone sealant on to the bottle using a pencil or pointed stick to form a simple line drawing, such as a series of swirls.

2 Cut white vitreous glass into small pieces, about 2mm (⅛in) and 4mm (⅛in), using tile nippers.

3 Stick these cut tesserae to the lines drawn in silicone sealant, then leave overnight to dry.

4 Choose an assortment of colours from the vitreous glass and cut them into quarters. Some of the quarters will have to be cut across the diagonal, so that they can fit between the white swirls. Stick to the bottle in a series of bands of colour with silicone sealant. Leave overnight to dry.

5 Mix up some cement-based tile adhesive. Wearing rubber gloves, rub the cement into the surface of the bottle. Make sure all the crevices between the tesserae are filled, otherwise the tesserae are liable to pull away, as silicone sealant remains rubbery. Wipe off excess cement with a dry soft cloth and leave overnight to dry.

6 If necessary, sand the bottle down and polish with a soft cloth.

Materials and Equipment You Will Need
Wine bottle · Silicone sealant · Pencil or pointed stick · Vitreous glass mosaic tiles, including white · Tile nippers ·
Cement-based tile adhesive · Mixing container · Rubber gloves · Abrasive paper (optional) · Soft cloth

LAMP STAND

The simple spiral pattern used to create this tall, elegant lamp stand follows the one that is already present on the cardboard tube used as a base. Pieces of mirror have been added to catch the light, and they sparkle when the lamp is switched on. The cardboard base is inherently light and therefore too unstable to be used as a lamp stand on its own, so plaster has been poured into the bottom to give it more weight and a lower centre of gravity. If plaster seems too messy, you could use modelling clay or sand instead.

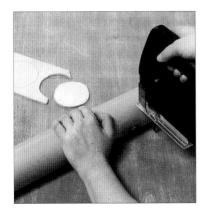

1 Draw twice around the circular end of the cardboard tube on to 4mm (⅛in) plywood. Cut around these circles using a jigsaw and cut the cardboard tube to the length required. Drill a hole through the centre of one of the plywood circles. Use a bradawl to make a hole in the cardboard tube 2cm (¾in) from one end and large enough to take the power cord.

2 Use wood glue to stick the plywood circle without the drilled hole to the end of the tube with the power cord hole. Leave overnight to dry, then paint the cardboard tube with shellac.

3 Thread the power cord through the hole in the cardboard tube and the hollow metal rod. Stand the metal rod inside the tube with the screw thread at the top. Mix some plaster of Paris with water and quickly pour it into the tube. Slip the second plywood circle over the metal rod and secure it with wood glue to the top of the cardboard tube. As soon as you have poured the plaster into the tube, you must work quickly to secure the top, as it is very important that the plaster dries with the rod in the upright position. Leave overnight to dry.

▶

Materials and Equipment You Will Need

Pencil · Cardboard carpet roll tube · 4mm (⅛in) plywood sheet · Jigsaw (saber saw) · Drill and bit · Bradawl · Wood glue · Shellac · Paintbrush · Length of power cord · Hollow metal rod with a screw thread, the length of the finished stand · Plaster of Paris · Mixing container · Tiles in three colours · Tile nippers · Cement-based tile adhesive · Sponge · Mirror · Rubber gloves · Flexible knife · Abrasive paper · Soft cloth · Copper tubing · Hacksaw · Lamp fittings · Plug · Screwdriver · Lampshade

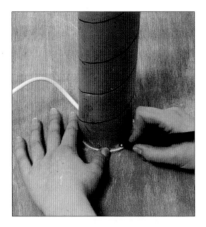

4 With a pencil, draw the design on to the tube, following the spiral lines that are already present on the cardboard tube. You could add additional variations and embellishments at this stage.

6 Select two colours of tile to fill the areas between the spiralling lines. Use the tile nippers to cut the tiles into various shapes and sizes. Cut the mirror into various shapes and sizes.

8 Wearing rubber gloves and using a flexible knife, apply wet cement-based tile adhesive over the whole area of the lamp stand, taking care to press it between all the tesserae. Wipe off the excess cement with a sponge and leave to dry overnight. Rub off any remaining surface cement with abrasive paper, and polish with a soft cloth.

5 Cut the tiles for the outline colour into small pieces using tile nippers. Stick these to the lines of your design using cement-based tile adhesive. Use a sponge to wipe away any large blobs of cement that seep out from under the tesserae, and leave to dry overnight.

7 Spread cement-based tile adhesive on to the remaining cardboard area, and apply the tesserae in separate bands of colour. Work on a small area at a time, so that the surface does not become too messy. Intersperse the coloured tesserae with pieces of mirror as you work. Cover the whole of the cardboard tube, then leave to dry overnight.

9 Finish off by attaching all the fittings. Slip copper tubing, cut to size, over the central rod, leaving the screw end exposed. Attach the lamp fittings, plug and lampshade.

STORAGE CHEST

This simple store-bought chest with drawers has been transformed by mosaic motifs into an individual, playful piece of furniture. Although you may not be able to find exactly the same chest, with a few modifications the basic ideas can be translated to another piece of furniture. Many white tesserae are used here, held together with white cement, to give the shelf a fresh, clean look that would make it suitable for a bathroom or child's bedroom. When tackling a piece of furniture that has movable parts such as doors and drawers, you need to be very careful that the tesserae do not impede the movement of the components once they are applied and grouted.

1 Paint the shelf and drawers inside and out with watered-down white undercoat. Leave to dry.

2 Draw a simple motif on the front of each drawer. Choose motifs that have a bold outline and are easily recognizable when executed in one colour.

3 Cut the tiles into unevenly shaped tesserae using tile nippers. Mix up some cement-based tile adhesive, spread it within the outline of one of the motifs, then firmly press single-coloured tesserae into it.

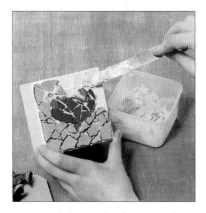

4 Surround the motif with tesserae of a different colour. Take care not to overlap the edges of the drawer. Cover the remaining drawer fronts using a different combination of two colours each time. ▶

Materials and Equipment You Will Need

Store-bought shelf with drawers • White undercoat • Paintbrush • Pencil • Thin tiles in five colours, plus white • Tile nippers • White cement-based tile adhesive • Mixing container • Flexible knife • Rubber gloves • Sponge • Abrasive paper • Square-bottomed paint scraper

5 Cut tiny slivers of white tile. Stick these to the narrow front edges of the chest with the tile adhesive. Do this very carefully so that none of the tesserae overlaps the edge.

6 Cut more white tiles into various shapes and sizes, then stick these to the large, flat outside surfaces of the shelf. When all four are covered, leave the shelf and the drawers to dry overnight.

7 Rub tile adhesive into the surface of the chest and drawers, wearing rubber gloves. Take special care when smoothing the cement into the thin edges of the shelf and the edges of the drawer fronts, making sure the cement is flush with the edges. When the gaps between the tesserae are filled, wipe off most of the excess cement with a sponge. Leave the chest to dry for 24 hours.

8 Sand off any remaining surface cement from the shelf and drawers. Then use an implement with a sharp, flat edge, such as a paint scraper, to scrape along the inside edge of the shelf and the sides of the drawers. Do this carefully to ensure there are no overlapping tesserae and there is no cement remaining to impede the action of the drawers.

CLOCK

This mosaic clockface is decorated with tesserae made from hand-painted Mexican tiles in shades of blue, brown and cream. Pretty shells have been used here to mark the quarter hours, although they are not absolutely necessary. While the painting on the tiles is very free-style and the tiles have been cut into uneven shapes, the resulting tesserae are used to construct a precise geometric shape. When designing a clock, you must first find a way of accommodating the mechanism that works the hands. Then you must design the surface decoration to accommodate the function of the clock. The base of this clock is made from two pieces of wood; the thicker piece at the back has a circular hole cut into it, large enough to accommodate the workings and batteries. As the clock must be easy to read, the tesserae are laid in a very simple and precise design. In fact, the primary function of the design, as with any clock, is to draw attention to the position of the hands.

1 Using a jigsaw, cut 4mm (⅛in) plywood and 2cm (¾in) chipboard into circles of the same diameter; the circles shown here are 40cm (16in) in diameter. Drill a hole through the centre of the chipboard circle, large enough to take the blade of the jigsaw. Saw a hole large enough to accommodate the clock's workings. Drill a hole through the centre of the plywood circle, large enough to take the pivot for the clock's hands. Prime both pieces with diluted PVA glue and allow to dry.

2 Stick the plywood and chipboard circles together with strong wood glue. Clamp the pieces together with cramps; if you don't have any cramps, you can use weights such as heavy books. Leave overnight to dry.

3 Draw a circle in the centre of the plywood circle. Its radius must be the length of the longest hand of the clock. Using a felt-tipped pen or pencil, section the face into quarters and use these as a basis for your design.

Materials and Equipment You Will Need
Jigsaw (saber saw) • 4mm (⅛in) plywood sheet • 2cm (¾in) chipboard (particle board) • Drill and bits • Clock fittings (battery-operated motor with a long pivotal pin, and hands) • PVA (white) glue • Paintbrush • Strong wood glue • Cramps (at least four) or heavy weights • Felt-tipped pen or pencil • Selection of plain and patterned tiles • Tile nippers • Cement-based tile adhesive • Mixing container • Flexible knife • Shells to mark quarter hours (optional) • Rubber gloves • Sponge • Abrasive paper • Soft cloth

4 Cut plain tiles into small, roughly rectangular shapes using tile nippers. Mix up some cement-based tile adhesive with water and apply to the edge using a flexible knife. Press the tesserae firmly into the cement.

5 Cut patterned tiles into small irregular shapes. This design uses three kinds of patterned tiles.

6 Tile the surface within the rotation area of the clock's arms, using cement-based tile adhesive applied to a small area at a time, so as not to obliterate the guidelines. Take care to lay the tesserae flat, as they must not impede the rotation of the clock's hands.

7 Tile the border, marking the positions of the quarter hours. Here, shells are used, but whatever you choose, it must not overlap the area where the hands rotate. Leave overnight to dry.

8 Using a flexible knife, smooth cement-based tile adhesive between the tesserae around the edge of the clockface.

9 Wearing rubber gloves, rub cement-based tile adhesive over the surface of the clockface. Make sure all the gaps between the tesserae are filled, then wipe clean with a sponge. Leave to dry for 24 hours.

▶

10 Sand off any excess cement and polish with a soft cloth.

11 Attach the components of the clock's workings. The battery-operated workings should fit into the hole at the back. Fix the pivotal pin through the hole in the centre, then fit the hands over this and secure with a nut.

POT STAND

As well as protecting your table top, this mosaic pot stand by Sarah Round will brighten up any meal time. The mosaic is stuck on to a board that has been cut into a geometric shape. This shape is integral to the pattern in which the tesserae are laid. The tesserae used here are cut carefully from brightly coloured tiles. Small chips are added to provide highlights to the areas of darkest colour. Black tile grout is used, but if you cannot get hold of this, you could colour ordinary tile grout with black ink.

1 Carefully mark the proportions of the pot stand on to a square piece of chipboard; use a ruler to make sure the lines are perfectly straight.

2 Prime both sides of the chipboard with diluted PVA glue and leave to dry. Cut around the outline of the design using a jigsaw. Sand down any rough edges and prime with diluted PVA glue. Leave to dry.

3 Decide on your colour scheme. Using tile nippers, cut the tiles into small pieces that will fit inside the shapes you have drawn. Here small pieces of mirror have been added to the dark blue sections of the mosaic, and small pieces of the dark blue tiles have been included in the lighter areas. Fix them in position with tile adhesive using a flexible knife. When the surface is covered, remove any excess tile adhesive with a sponge and leave to dry for 24 hours.

4 Fill the gaps between the tesserae with black tile grout. Rub the grout into the sides of the stand as well, then leave to dry for about 10 minutes. Wipe off any excess grout with a sponge, then leave to dry for 24 hours. Paint the sides of the pot stand with diluted PVA glue. Cut felt to size and stick it to the back of the stand with PVA glue. Finish by polishing the top surface with a soft cloth and clear glass polish.

Materials and Equipment You Will Need
1cm (½in) chipboard (particle board), 30 x 30cm (12 x12in) • Pencil • Ruler • PVA (white) glue • Paintbrush • Jigsaw (saber saw) • Abrasive paper • Tiles in three colours • Tile nippers • Mirror • Tile adhesive • Mixing container • Flexible knife • Black ready-mixed tile grout • Grout spreader • Sponge • Felt • Scissors • Soft cloth • Clear glass polish

COAT RACK

Storage of coats is always a problem, but if they have to be hung in a hall or room, make the rack an interesting feature rather than a necessary evil. Sandra Hadfield has decorated this home-made rack with brightly coloured vitreous glass tesserae. These are cut into a variety of shapes and sizes and fixed to the base using the direct method, to form bold outlines and blocks of colour. The base of the rack can be made from medium-density wood, which can be cut into any size and shape you like.

1 Cut a piece of MDF or plywood to the length required. Draw the outline of the top on to this base using a pencil and ruler to make sure the proportions are correct. Cut around the outline using a jigsaw. Sand down any rough edges.

2 Attach two mirror plates to the back of the base, one at each end. Make sure the screw holes stick out far enough from the sides of the base; when the sides are tiled with the tesserae, the holes must remain uncovered.

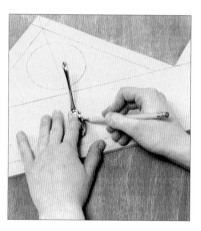

3 Draw the mosaic design on to the surface of the base. Position the coat hooks and draw around them on to the base.

Materials and Equipment You Will Need
1cm (½in) MDF (medium-density fiberboard) or plywood sheet • Saw • Pencil • Ruler • Jigsaw (saber saw) • Abrasive paper • 2 mirror plates • Screws • Screwdriver • 3 coat hooks • Sharp knife • PVA (white) glue • Medium and fine paintbrushes • Mixing container • Vitreous glass mosaic tiles • Tile nippers • Rubber gloves • Ready-mixed tile grout • Grout spreader • Sponge • Nailbrush • Soft cloth

4 Score the base with a sharp knife and prime the front, back and sides with diluted PVA glue.

5 Here, whole blue vitreous glass tiles are alternated with half tiles around the border. Cut the tiles using tile nippers. Fix the outlining tesserae along the outside edge of the base with PVA glue applied with a fine paintbrush.

6 Stick tesserae to the areas between the main outlines. Cover the entire surface, except for the areas where the hooks will be screwed in. Cut in half vitreous glass tiles of the same colour as the outlines and carefully stick them along the edges of the base. Leave to dry for 24 hours.

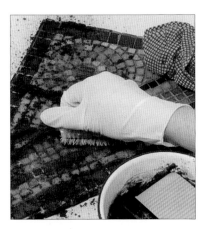

7 Wearing rubber gloves, spread grout over the surface of the mosaic, pushing it into the gaps between the tesserae. Wipe off the excess grout with a sponge and leave for about 10 minutes, so that the surface dries. Then use a stiff nailbrush to scrub off any grout that has dried on the surface of the mosaic. Leave to dry for 24 hours.

8 Sand off any remaining grout on the surface of the mosaic, then polish with a soft cloth. Screw the coat hooks into position, and hang in place.

HEART MIRROR

Sarah Round has designed a bold, playful mosaic surround for this mirror, with a crown motif along the top edge and a mosaic heart hanging from the bottom. The majority of the tesserae are made from white tiles that have been individually fashioned to fit into one another. The heart is tiled with tesserae cut from blue and yellow tiles. These colours are also used for the spots of colour in the points along the top of the mirror. The use of black grout gives a stirring effect by strongly emphasizing the edges and shapes of the white tesserae. Black grout can be difficult to find, but you can make your own by mixing black ink into white grout powder.

1 Draw the outline of the frame and the position of the mirror on a piece of 1cm (½in) chipboard. Draw the outline for the heart, which will hang from the bottom. Prime the chipboard with diluted PVA glue. Cut around the shapes using a handsaw or jigsaw. Sand any rough edges, then prime as before.

2 Cut three small circles from the tiles using tile nippers. To do this, cut the tiles into small squares, then nibble the corners away. Fix the circles in position along the top edge of the frame using tile adhesive. Lay the background tiles on the frame and mark the cutting lines with a washable felt-tipped pen.

3 Cut along the marked lines with the tile nippers.

4 Fix the cut tiles in position with tile adhesive. Work around the frame, cutting and sticking the tesserae one at a time. In this way, you can cut the tesserae individually to fit neatly. ▶

Materials and Equipment You Will Need

1cm (½in) chipboard (particle board) • Mirror • Pencil • Ruler • PVA (white) glue • Paintbrush • Handsaw or jigsaw (saber saw) • Abrasive paper • Tiles in three colours • Tile nippers • Tile adhesive • Washable felt-tipped pen • Sponge • Epoxy resin glue (optional) • Black ready-mixed tile grout • Grout spreader • Soft cloth • Clear glass polish • Paper or felt • Hanging clip (D-ring) • Bradawl • Pliers • Thick wire, such as coat-hanger wire

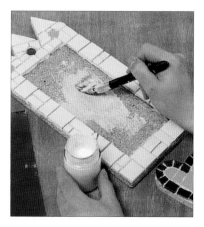

5 Remove any excess tile adhesive from the surface or sides of the mosaic with a sponge. Fix the mirror into position with PVA or epoxy resin glue. Leave to dry for 24 hours.

6 Spread black tile grout over the surface of the frame and heart with a grout spreader, pushing it into all the gaps between the tesserae.

7 Spread grout on to the sides of the frame and heart.

8 Leave to dry for 10 minutes, then wipe off any excess grout with a sponge. Leave the mirror and heart to dry for a further 24 hours, then polish the surface with a soft dry cloth and clear glass polish.

9 Paint the edges of the mirror and heart with diluted PVA glue. Stick either paper or felt on to the back of the mirror, and fix a hanging clip. Leave to dry. Using a bradawl, make a hole in the middle of the bottom edge of the mirror frame and in the centre of the top edge of the heart. Use pliers to cut a piece of thick wire about 6cm (2½in) long.

10 Apply epoxy resin glue to both ends of the wire and to the holes made in the mirror and heart. Push the wire into these holes and leave to dry fully before attempting to move the mirror.

BATHROOM CABINET

In this witty visual pun, Norma Vondee has decorated the door of a bathroom cabinet with a trompe l'œil mosaic, behind which can be hidden the clutter of bathroom pills and potions. The shadows and highlights give the bottle, glass and pot the illusion of being three-dimensional. Use this project to practise classic mosaic techniques. When laying the mosaic, pay close attention to the position of each of the tesserae and the patterns formed by the gaps left between them. The tesserae used are cinca ceramic mosaic tiles, available in a wide range of colours. They have a soft matt texture and are very easy to cut and shape, so are perfect when experimenting with precise mosaics.

1 Remove the panel in the door of the cabinet. Cut a 4mm (⅛in) plywood panel to the same size. Score the surface with a sharp knife to provide a key for the PVA glue. Draw your design on the plywood, using a template if required. Mark in the ellipses and areas of shadow.

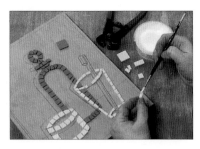

2 Cut the cinca mosaic tiles into precise shapes using tile nippers. Apply these

tesserae to the main outlines, fixing them in place with PVA glue. Take extra care when tiling curved areas.

3 Carefully fill the areas inside the outlines in contrasting colours. Here, reflections and highlights are depicted using different shades of tesserae to create the illusion of a three-dimensional scene. Use tesserae a shade darker than the background to tile areas of shadow.

4 Outline the shapes with a row of tesserae in the background colour. If making a larger design, you could use a double row of tesserae to outline the subjects of the mosaic.

5 Fill in the background colour with tesserae arranged in straight lines and leave overnight to dry. Secure the panel in position on the cabinet door and mask the frame with tape. Mix three parts sand and one part cement with water and a little red cement dye. Grout the mosaic with this mixture using a squeegee. Clean the surface carefully with a soft cloth and leave to dry as slowly as possible.

Materials and Equipment You Will Need
Wall-mounted cabinet with door • 4mm (⅛in) plywood sheet • Saw • Sharp knife • Pencil • Paper for template (optional) • Cinca ceramic tiles • Tile nippers • PVA (white) glue • Fine paintbrush • Masking tape • Sand • Cement • Red cement dye • Mixing container • Squeegee • Soft cloth

SPLASHBACK

Mosaic is an ideal decorative surface or wall cladding for areas in which water is present, such as this splashback for a bathroom sink. It is made by applying roughly broken tiles in subtle colours, and chips of glass to catch the light, directly on to a plywood base.

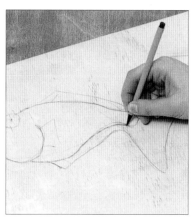

1 Measure the width of your sink and cut 4mm (⅛in) plywood to size. Prime the surface with PVA adhesive. When dry, draw a simple fish design on the plywood.

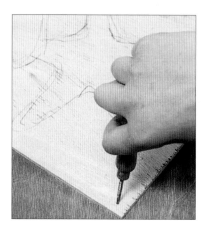

2 Using a bradawl, make a hole through the plywood in each corner.

3 Select the colours of the tiles to be used for tesserae; here, two similar greys are used for the fish and a muted pink for the starfish. Wear goggles or, alternatively, cover the tiles with a heavy cloth, then using a hammer, smash the tiles into a variety of shapes.

Materials and Equipment You Will Need

Tape measure • 4mm (⅛in) plywood sheet • Saw • PVA (white) glue • Paintbrush • Pencil • Bradawl • Tiles in several colours • Goggles or heavy cloth • Hammer • Tile nippers • Cement-based tile adhesive • Mixing container • Flexible knife • Thin edging tiles • Mirror • Spoon • Soft brush • Plant mister • Drinking straw • Scissors • Abrasive paper • Soft cloth • Drill • Wall plugs • 4 mirror screws • Screwdriver

4 Select a suitable tile that has a soft base with a thin glaze, such as a Mexican tile. Using the tile nippers, nibble two circles for the eyes of the fish. Use a bradawl to carefully make a hole in the centre of each.

6 When the fish and starfish are complete, smash tiles of the background colour, in this case a soft blue. Spread cement-based tile adhesive on to the base, a small area at a time. Press the background tesserae firmly into the cement. Be careful not to tile over the holes that you have made in the corners.

8 Using tile nippers, cut the mirror into small pieces. Press these tesserae into the larger gaps in the design, on top of a blob of cement to keep them level with the other tesserae. Leave to dry for 24 hours.

5 Mix up some tile adhesive with water and spread it on to the base within the outlines of your drawing. Fix the tesserae within the drawn lines, using a lighter shade for the fins and tail and the darker shade for the body of the fish. Try to find tesserae in shapes that will fit within the drawing and suggest the movement of the fish.

7 Cut thin edging tiles into short segments and fix them around the edge of the mosaic.

9 Spoon dry tile adhesive on to the surface of the splashback and brush it into the cracks using a soft brush. Avoid the area around the hole in each corner. ▶

10 Spray the surface with plenty of water using a plant mister.

11 Cut a drinking straw into four pieces and stand one over each hole in the corner. Mix up some tile adhesive and grout around the straws. Leave to dry for 12 hours.

12 Remove the straws and sand off any cement remaining on the surface of the splashback, then polish with a soft cloth. Place the splashback against the wall and mark the positions of the screw holes. Drill the holes and insert wall plugs. Use mirror screws with metal caps to screw the splashback in position.

FIRE SCREEN

In this project, mosaic is used to decorate a ready-made fire screen, which can be purchased at good craft suppliers.
Alternatively, a simple screen shape can be cut from plywood using a jigsaw, and slotted into custom-made feet.
For her bold design Sandra Hadfield has used vitreous glass mosaic tiles in striking colours. Most of this design
uses whole tiles, cut diagonally into triangles.

1 Draw the design on the surface of the fire screen and its feet. Calculate the amount of space needed to accommodate the tiles required and use a ruler to mark the main areas. Score the surface with a sharp knife, then prime with diluted PVA glue and leave to dry.

2 Select vitreous glass tiles in the colours you require. Cut some tiles into triangles for the border.

3 Fix the tesserae to the base with PVA glue. Try to make all of the gaps between the tesserae equal and leave the area that will be slotted into the feet untiled.

4 Tile the edge, then the feet, making sure they will still slot on to the screen. Leave overnight to dry. Wearing rubber gloves, rub grout into the surface of the mosaic, making sure all the gaps between the tesserae are filled. Leave to dry for about 10 minutes, then remove any excess grout with a nailbrush. Allow the grout to dry for a further 12 hours, then paint the back of the screen with wood primer, undercoat and finally gloss paint, allowing each coat to dry before applying the next. Polish the mosaic with a soft cloth and slot on the feet.

▶

Materials and Equipment You Will Need
Ready-made fire screen base • Pencil • Ruler • Sharp knife • PVA (white) glue • Paintbrushes • Vitreous glass mosaic tiles • Tile nippers •
Rubber gloves • Ready-mixed tile grout • Nailbrush • Wood primer • White undercoat • Gloss paint • Soft cloth

LOVE LETTER RACK

Personal letters and correspondence often have a tendency to be misplaced or lost in a busy household. Tessa Brown's simple but effective design for a letter rack could be the answer to this perennial problem. She has used heart motifs, but any simple patterns or shapes could be substituted. The rack is a simple construction. Pieces of medium-density fibreboard are cut to shape using a jigsaw or coping saw. The front is decorated with vitreous glass tesserae, which have been cut carefully to fit the design.

1 Draw the shapes of the components of the rack on to both pieces of MDF or plywood. Cut them out with a jigsaw. Prime the surfaces with diluted PVA glue. When dry, draw the pattern on to the front panel. Stick the pieces together with wood glue. Secure with panel pins. Leave to dry overnight.

2 Select two tones of red tiles. Using tile nippers, nibble into shapes to fit your design. Fix in position with cellulose filler.

3 Select the colours of vitreous glass to tile around the hearts. Trim the tesserae to fit snugly around the motif and within the edges of the rack. Fix them to the base. Leave to dry overnight.

4 Smooth cellulose filler over the surface of the mosaic.

5 Rub the filler into all the gaps with your fingers. Rub off any excess filler with a damp sponge and leave to dry. Use abrasive paper to remove any filler that has dried on the surface of the mosaic and to neaten the edges.

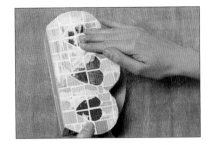

6 Paint the parts of the rack that are not covered with mosaic with red paint. Leave to dry.

Materials and Equipment You Will Need

4mm (⅛in) and 1cm (½in) MDF (medium-density fiberboard) or plywood sheet • Pencil • Jigsaw (saber saw) • PVA (white) glue • Paintbrushes • Wood glue • Panel pins (brads) • Pin hammer • Vitreous glass mosaic tiles • Tile nippers • White cellulose filler • Grout spreader or flexible knife • Sponge • Abrasive paper • Red paint

MIRROR

Mosaic is a very effective way of surrounding a mirror. The undulating, fractured surface created by the tesserae perfectly sets off the smooth, reflective plane of the glass. This mirror, designed by Cleo Mussi, has an attractive frame to add interest and atmosphere to a bathroom. She has chosen to use china with delicate patterns in cool, fresh colours and with touches of gold.

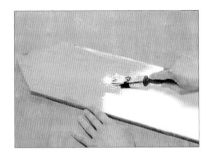

1 Draw the outer shape of the mirror frame on to a piece of 2cm (¾in) plywood. Cut around this shape using a jigsaw, then sand down the rough edges. On to this base panel, draw the desired shape of the mirror glass. Here, the shape of the mirror glass echoes the shape of the panel, but it could be a completely different shape if desired. Make sure it is a shape that glass-cutters will be able to reproduce.

2 Seal the sides and front of the base panel with diluted PVA glue and paint the back first with wood primer, then undercoat and finally gloss varnish. Mark the position of the mirror plate on the back of the panel. Using an appropriate drill bit, rebate (rabbet) the area that will be under the keyhole-shaped opening (large enough to take a screw head). Then screw the mirror plate in position.

3 Make a card template in the exact dimensions of the mirror shape you have drawn on the base. Ask your supplier to cut a piece of 4mm (⅛in) foil-backed mirror using your template.

4 Stick the mirror in position using ready-mixed tile adhesive. Leave to dry overnight. ▶

Materials and Equipment You Will Need
2cm (¾in) plywood sheet • Pencil • Ruler • Jigsaw (saber saw) • Abrasive paper • PVA (white) glue • Paintbrushes • Wood primer • White undercoat • Gloss varnish • Drill with rebating (rabbeting) bit • Mirror plate • 2 2cm (¾in) screws • Screwdriver • Cardboard • 4mm (⅛in) foil-backed mirror • Tile adhesive • Flexible knife • Masking tape • Tracing paper (optional) • Tile nippers • Selection of china • Powdered tile grout • Vinyl matt emulsion or acrylic paint (optional) • Mixing container • Grout spreader or rubber gloves • Nailbrush • Soft cloth

5 Trim 2mm (¹⁄₁₆in) from the template all around the edge and cover the mirror with it, securing it in place with masking tape; this should prevent the mirror from being scratched. The mosaic will eventually overlap the 2mm (¹⁄₁₆in) of uncovered mirror.

6 Draw the design for the frame on the dry, sealed surface surrounding the mirror; use tracing paper and a soft pencil to copy and transfer your original plan, if you wish.

7 Using tile nippers, snip the smooth edges from the cups and plates you have collected. Use these to tile the outside edge of the base panel and to overlap the 2mm (¹⁄₁₆in) edges of the mirror, sticking them down with ready-mixed tile adhesive. Cut the remainder of the china into small pieces and stick these to the structural lines of your design.

8 Fill in the areas of detail between the outlining tesserae. When the mirror frame is completely tiled, leave it to dry for 24 hours.

9 Mix powdered tile grout with water and, if desired, colour with vinyl matt emulsion or acrylic paint. Spread this over the surface of the tesserae using a grout spreader or wear rubber gloves and rub it in by hand, making sure all the gaps between the tesserae have been filled. Allow the surface to dry for a few minutes, then brush off the excess grout with a stiff-bristled nailbrush. Wipe clean with a soft cloth.

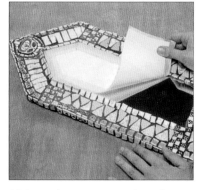

10 Leave the mirror overnight to dry thoroughly, then remove the protective card from the mirrored glass and hang it in position.

SKIRTING BOARD

A skirting (base) board is an unusual and discreet way of introducing mosaic into your home. You can use a repeated abstract design, a succession of motifs, or a combination of the two. Here, the motif of a daisy has been repeated at regular intervals. The tesserae are made from marble tiles that have been roughly broken with a hammer. You will need a large quantity of tiles, so it is best to use the skirting board to decorate a small room.

1 Measure the room and buy lengths of skirting board to fit. Roughen the surface with coarse-grade abrasive paper, then prime it with diluted PVA glue. Leave to dry.

2 Mark the skirting board into small, equally spaced sections. Using a dark pencil, draw a simple motif in each section. Here, the motif is a daisy.

4 Mix up some cement-based tile adhesive and, working on a small area at a time, spread it along the lines of your drawing. Press the broken pieces of marble firmly into the cement. Choose tesserae in shapes that echo those of the design, for example, the petal shapes of the flower. The marble can be roughly shaped by tapping the edges of larger tesserae with a hammer. When each motif is tiled, wipe off any excess cement with a sponge and leave to dry overnight. ▶

3 Wear goggles or cover the tiles with a cloth. Smash the marble tiles into small pieces with a hammer.

Materials and Equipment You Will Need
Ruler or tape measure • Skirting (base) board • Coarse-grade abrasive paper • PVA (white) glue • Paintbrush • Pencil • Goggles or cloth • Selection of marble tiles • Hammer • Cement-based tile adhesive • Mixing container • Flexible knife • Sponge • Rubber gloves or squeegee • Abrasive paper • Soft cloth

5 Break up tiles in the background colour with a hammer. Working on a small area at a time, spread cement-based adhesive on to the untiled sections of skirting board and press the tesserae into it. When the surface is covered, use small pieces of the background colour to tile along the top edge of the skirting, ensuring that the tesserae do not overlap the edge. Leave to dry for 24 hours.

7 Sand off any cement that has dried on the surface of the mosaic and polish the surface with a soft cloth. Fix the skirting board in position.

6 Wearing rubber gloves or using a squeegee, rub wet cement-based adhesive into the surface of the mosaic, filling all the gaps between the tesserae. Use a flexible knife to spread the cement into the edge. Wipe off any excess with a cloth and leave overnight to dry.

AZTEC BOX

The Aztecs and Mayas of pre-Colombian Central America used to decorate skulls, weapons and snake shapes with precious materials such as turquoise, coral and jade. This decoration was intended to seal in the magical energies of the object and ward off evil. Norma Vondee was inspired by such treasures to make this mosaic jewellery box. For the tesserae she has used vitreous glass and cinca tiles in colours that echo those used by the Central American artists. She has also included glass globules backed with gold and silver leaf.

1 Draw the design with a felt-tipped pen or dark pencil. Here, the teeth of the beast are drawn below the opening edge of the lid.

2 Stick on glass globules for the eyes, holding in place with masking tape until dry. Cut vitreous glass tiles in coral and stick on to the nose and lips. Cut vitreous glass tiles in pink and terracotta to line the lips. Use a paintbrush to apply glue to small pieces.

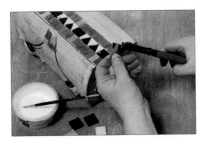

3 Cut black and white tesserae into precise shapes to fit the areas marked for the teeth, then stick them in position.

4 Select tesserae in varying shades of turquoise, blue and green, and use them to tile around the eye sockets and to delineate the snout, cutting them where necessary to fit the sides of the box. Include a few small glass globules positioned randomly.

5 When tiling around the hinges, leave about 1cm (½in) untiled, so that the box can be opened easily. Leave to dry, then tile the lid in the same way.

6 Mix three parts sand with one part cement and add a little black cement dye. Add water a little at a time until the desired consistency is attained. Wearing rubber gloves, rub the cement on to the surface of the box. Scrape off the excess cement with a squeegee, then rub the box with a slightly damp sponge. Finish by polishing with a dry cloth, then cover the box with a plastic bag so that it will dry as slowly as possible.

Materials and Equipment You Will Need
Wooden box with hinged lid • Felt-tipped pen or dark pencil • Glass globules backed with gold and silver leaf • PVA (white) glue • Masking tape • Mixing containers • Fine paintbrush • Vitreous glass mosaic tiles • Tile nippers • Cinca ceramic tiles • Sand • Cement • Black cement dye • Rubber gloves • Squeegee • Sponge • Soft cloth • Plastic bag

GARDEN TABLE

The bold design of this table top and the simplicity and delicacy of the metal frame that supports it combine to create a table that would look good in the conservatory, or as an occasional table for a garden or patio on a sunny day. The top is decorated with tesserae made from roughly broken floor tiles, which have a strong texture. Highlights are created by the inclusion of tiny chips of gold-leaf smalti. The metal frame used here was made to order by a local blacksmith, and there are many such craftspeople willing to make one-off pieces of this kind. Alternatively, frames can often be found in secondhand furniture stores.

1 Draw the shape of the table top on a piece of 2cm (¾in) plywood. Cut this out using a jigsaw and sand off any rough edges. Then prime with diluted PVA glue, paying special attention to the edges.

2 Draw a simple design on the table top. You may need to use a tape measure to get the proportions right, but don't be too rigid about the geometry, as a freehand approach suits this method of working.

3 Cut floor tiles in your outlining colour into small pieces using tile nippers. Try to cut them into a variety of shapes; uniform shapes would jar with the crazy paving effect of the smashed tesserae used for the rest of the table.

Materials and Equipment You Will Need

2cm (¾in) plywood sheet • Pencil • Jigsaw (saber saw) • PVA (white) glue • Paintbrush • Tape measure (optional) • Selection of floor tiles • Tile nippers • Cement-based tile adhesive • Mixing containers • Flexible knife • Sponge • Goggles or cloth • Hammer • Gold-leaf tesserae • Spoon • Soft brush • Plant mister • Abrasive paper • Dilute hydrochloric acid (optional) • Rubber gloves (optional) • Metal table frame • Screws • Screwdriver • Soft cloth

4 Mix up some cement-based tile adhesive and, using a flexible knife, spread it around the edge of the table top. Firmly press the outlining tesserae into the cement, making sure they do not overlap the edges.

5 Apply the cement-based tile adhesive to the lines of your drawing and press in the outlining tesserae. Use a sponge to wipe away any large bits of cement that have squashed out from under the edges of the tesserae and leave overnight to dry.

6 Wear goggles or cover the tiles with a cloth. Using a hammer, smash the tiles that are to fill in the areas between the outlines.

7 Apply cement-based tile adhesive to small areas of the table top at a time and press in the tile fragments. Do this carefully as the finished surface needs to be as flat as possible. Leave overnight for the cement to dry.

8 Using a flexible knife, smooth cement-based tile adhesive on to the edges of the table.

9 Cut gold-leaf tesserae into tiny, irregular shapes using tile nippers. Place these in the larger gaps between the broken tiles on the table top. If necessary, first insert a blob of cement adhesive to ensure that the gold is at the same level as the tiles. Leave to dry overnight. ▶

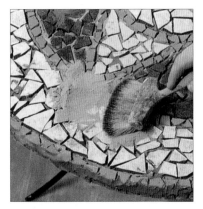

10 Spoon dry cement-based adhesive on to the surface of the table. Smooth it over the surface with a soft brush, making sure all the gaps between the tesserae have been filled. Spray water over the table using a plant mister. When the cement has absorbed enough water, wipe away any excess with a cloth. If the cement sinks when wetted, repeat the whole process. Leave to dry for 24 hours. Turn the table top over and rub wet cement-based tile adhesive into the plywood on the underside. Leave overnight to dry.

11 Clean off any excess cement with abrasive paper. Alternatively, dilute hydrochloric acid can be used but you must wear goggles and rubber gloves and apply it outside or where there is good ventilation. Wash any acid residue from the surface.

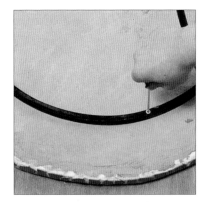

12 When clean, turn the table top face down and screw the metal frame in place using screws that are no longer than the thickness of the plywood. Polish the table top with a soft cloth.

FLOWERPOT

For this flowerpot, combining both the functional and decorative qualities of mosaics, Cleo Mussi has chosen a design and colours that reflect the flowers to be planted in it. Small squares of mirror are included in the design, as they will reflect the dappled light of a leafy garden or conservatory (sun room). As only part of the pot is to be covered with mosaic, a ready-glazed, high-fired terracotta pot is used. This is especially important if the pot is to be left outside all year. Alternatively, if the whole of the outer surface of a pot is to be covered in mosaic, a frost-resistant terracotta pot may be used, as long as the pot is waterproofed on the inside by sealing it with PVA (white) glue.

1 Draw a simple design on the pot, using chalk or a wax crayon.

2 Cut appropriate shapes from the china using tile nippers. Mix up some cement-based tile adhesive and use it to fix the tesserae to the pot with a flexible knife.

3 Work first on the main lines and detailed areas, applying the adhesive to small areas at a time so that you can follow the lines of the design.

4 Fill in the larger areas of plain colour. When complete, leave the pot to dry for 24 hours.

5 Mix powdered grout with water and a little cement dye. Wearing rubber gloves, spread the grout over the pot, filling all the cracks between the tesserae. Allow the surface to dry, then brush off any excess grout with a nailbrush. Allow the pot to dry for at least 48 hours before polishing with a dry soft cloth.

Materials and Equipment You Will Need
Flowerpot • Chalk or wax crayon • Selection of china • Tile nippers • Cement-based tile adhesive • Mixing container • Flexible knife • Powdered waterproof tile grout • Cement dye • Rubber gloves • Nailbrush • Soft cloth

DECORATIVE SPHERES

Cleo Mussi was inspired by millefiori African beadwork to make these mosaic spheres. Use them as unusual garden decorations, or fill a bowl with them for a striking table centrepiece. You could select fragments of china in colours that reflect the season, for example: citrus colours for a fresh spring feel; Mediterranean blues, white and terracotta for summer; golds, rusts and rich berry colours for the autumn; white, greys and black with lots of mirror for the winter months. The bases used for these spheres can be wood or polystyrene. If polystyrene is used, the spheres remain very light and would make effective hanging decorations, such as Christmas tree baubles or mobiles.

1 Seal the polystyrene or wooden spheres with diluted PVA glue. Leave to dry.

3 Combine different sizes of tesserae. Stick the pieces to the sphere with a waterproof tile adhesive. Leave to dry overnight.

5 Leave for a few minutes until the surface has dried, then brush off any excess grout using a stiff nailbrush.

2 Roughly draw a simple design on to a sphere using a pencil. A combination of circular motifs and stripes works well, but you can experiment with other geometric shapes and abstract designs. Cut the china and mirror into pieces, using tile nippers.

4 Mix grout with water and a little coloured vinyl matt emulsion or acrylic paint. Wearing rubber gloves, rub the grout into the surface of the sphere, filling all the cracks between the tesserae.

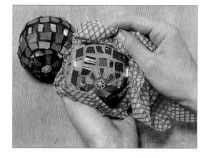

6 Leave to dry overnight, then polish with a dry soft cloth. Allow the spheres to air for a few days before arranging.

Materials and Equipment You Will Need

10 polystyrene (Styrofoam) or wooden spheres • PVA (white) glue • Paintbrush • Pencil • Selection of china • Mirror • Tile nippers • Tile adhesive • Powdered tile grout • Mixing container • Vinyl matt emulsion or acrylic paint • Rubber gloves • Nailbrush • Soft cloth

CHINA TILES

If you would like to introduce mosaic to an outdoor setting but are daunted by a large project, these one-off tiles by Cleo Mussi are the perfect solution. They could be fixed to a wall as an interesting feature or displayed alongside other garden decorations. You could stick a few tiles to your wall, each in a different colour or design, or repeat the same pattern at regular intervals. The tiles can also be used as table mats or coasters. This is a good project to choose for your first attempt at using china as tesserae. Don't be too exacting with your initial attempts, rather think of them as sketches or experiments before embarking upon larger, more complex mosaics.

1 Prime the back of a plain tile with diluted PVA glue and leave to dry. Draw a simple design on the back of the tile using a pencil.

2 Cut a selection of china into small pieces that will fit into your design, using tile nippers. Arrange these tesserae in groups according to colour and shape.

3 Dip the tesserae into tile adhesive and press them, one by one, on to the tile, using the drawing as a guide. When you press them on to the tile, glue should ooze out around the tesserae. When the tile is covered with mosaic, leave it to dry overnight.

4 Mix acrylic paint or cement dye with powdered waterproof tile grout.

Add water and mix to a dough-like consistency. Wearing rubber gloves, rub the grout into the surface of the mosaic, making sure that all the gaps between the tesserae are filled. Leave to dry for about 10 minutes.

5 Scrub the surface of the tile with a stiff nailbrush to remove all the excess grout, which should come away as powder. When clean, leave the tile to dry for 24 hours. Finish the tile by polishing it with a soft cloth.

Materials and Equipment You Will Need
Plain white tiles • PVA (white) glue • Paintbrush • Pencil • Selection of china • Tile nippers • Tile adhesive • Mixing container • Acrylic paint or cement dye • Powdered waterproof tile grout • Rubber gloves • Nailbrush • Soft cloth

JAR NIGHT LIGHT

When lit with a small candle, this stained-glass night-light, designed by Tessa Brown, throws patches of coloured light across a room. One jar is used as the base and another is broken into fragments that are painted a variety of colours with stained-glass paints. These fragments are then stuck on to the base jar and the gaps between the glass are grouted. Ideally you should select two jars of the same size, but if you cannot find two exactly the same, use the smaller one as the base.

1 Wrap one of the jars in an old dish towel. Wearing goggles and protective gloves, and covering your hair, smash the jar with a hammer. If the jars are of different sizes, smash the larger one.

2 Pick pieces to use as tesserae. Place them on scrap paper with the sharp edges facing downwards to avoid cutting yourself. Wrap any unused glass in newspaper and dispose of it carefully.

3 Use reusable adhesive to pick up the broken pieces of glass and turn them over so that the sharp edges face upwards. Paint the concave surface of each fragment with stained-glass paint. Here, three colours are used. Leave the pieces to dry.

4 Glue the painted glass fragments to the base jar, using a transparent rapid-setting epoxy resin glue, which must be solvent-free. Leave to dry thoroughly.

5 Spread cellulose filler over the surface, making sure all the gaps are filled. Smooth into the top and bottom edges of the jar and wipe off most of the excess. Leave to dry. If the filler has settled and cracks have appeared, use more filler.

6 When dry, clean any excess filler with a scourer and water. Use abrasive paper to neaten the top and bottom edges. Colour the filler with acrylic paint.

Materials and Equipment You Will Need

2 glass jars • Old dish towel • Goggles • Protective gloves • Hammer • Scrap paper • Newspaper • Reusable adhesive • Stained-glass paints • Paintbrushes • Solvent-free, rapid setting transparent epoxy resin • White cellulose filler • Grout spreader • Scourer • Abrasive paper • Acrylic paint

STAR WALL MOTIFS

These little wall motifs have been created by Cleo Mussi to add sparkling focal points to a garden. They are particularly effective when displayed in clusters or surrounded by lush foliage. Using tesserae cut from china and glass, they can be made up in any shape, size or design and in as many quantities as you wish. These star mosaics have been stuck on to thin plywood bases so that they can be movable features. However, if desired, they can be made permanent simply by sticking the tesserae directly on to the wall surface.

1 Draw a star motif on 4mm (⅛in) plywood using a pencil and a T square, ruler and a pair of compasses.

2 Cut out the star using a coping saw or an electric scroll saw. Sand down any rough edges, then seal one side with diluted PVA glue.

3 Make two small holes through the star using a bradawl.

4 Paint the unsealed side with wood primer, then undercoat and finish with a coat of gloss or matt paint. Allow each coat to dry before applying the next.

5 Cut a short length of wire and bend it into a loop for hanging the star. Push the ends through the holes in the star from the painted side and secure them to the front with staples or tape.

▶

Materials and Equipment You Will Need

4mm (⅛in) plywood sheet • Pencil • T square • Ruler • Pair of compasses • Coping saw or electric scroll saw • Abrasive paper • PVA (white) glue • Paintbrushes • Bradawl • Wood primer • White undercoat • Gloss or matt paint • Wire cutters • Wire • Stapler or tape • Selection of china • Mirror • Tile nippers • Tile adhesive • Powdered tile grout • Cement dye • Mixing containers • Rubber gloves • Nailbrush • Soft cloth

6 Snip the china and mirror into small pieces using tile nippers and arrange these pieces into groups according to colour and shape.

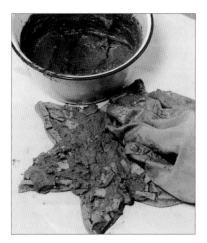

8 Mix the desired quantity of grout with cement dye. Adding a little water at a time, mix until the grout is of a dough-like consistency. Wearing rubber gloves, push the grout into all the gaps between the tesserae. Leave to dry for a few minutes.

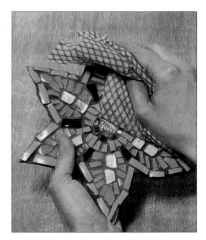

10 Polish the surface with a soft, dry cloth, then leave to dry for 24 hours before hanging outside.

7 Stick the china and mirror fragments to the surface of the star, one piece at a time. Take each fragment and dip it into ready-mixed tile adhesive, making sure enough is on the fragment to ooze a little from under the edges when pressed on to the base. Cover the surface of the star and leave overnight to dry.

9 Using a nailbrush, gently remove all the excess grout. This should brush away as powder; if it does not, the grout is still too damp, so leave to dry for a few more minutes before brushing again.

PRINCESS WALL MOSAIC

Gardens offer the mosaic artist the opportunity to experiment with more playful wall mosaics. There is less pressure to be 'tasteful', as the pieces can be softened by plants and garden bric-a-brac. This rather tongue-in-cheek princess design is applied to a wall using the semi-indirect method. This means that it can be made up in the comfort of your home or studio, then moved later, as a whole, and fixed to its base. It uses tesserae of vitreous glass in vibrant colours, which will not fade when exposed to the elements.

1 Scale up the template from the back of the book or draw a simple design on brown paper.

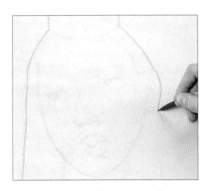

2 Make a tracing of the outline of your drawing and cut this out. You will use this later as a template to mark the area of the wall to be covered with cement.

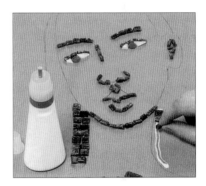

4 Stick these tesserae face down on to the main lines of your drawing using water-soluble glue. Stick down any key features, such as the eyes and lips, in contrasting colours.

3 Cut tiles in the outlining colour into eighths, using tile nippers.

Materials and Equipment You Will Need

Brown paper • Pencil • Tracing paper • Scissors • Vitreous glass mosaic tiles, including pink • Tile nippers • Water-soluble glue • Mirror • Board • Cement-based tile adhesive • Mixing container • Notched trowel • Sponge • Abrasive paper (optional) • Dilute hydrochloric acid (optional) • Goggles (optional) • Rubber gloves (optional) • Soft cloth

►

5 Cut pink vitreous glass tiles into quarters. Glue these face down to fill in the areas between the outlines.

6 Cut the mirror into small pieces about the same size as the quartered vitreous glass tesserae.

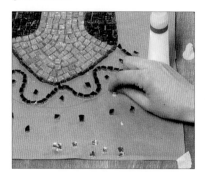

7 Stick the pieces of mirror face down on to the dress and in the crown.

8 Cut the tiles for the dress and the crown into quarters and glue them face down between the pieces of mirror. Leave the paper-backed mosaic to dry securely in position.

9 Transfer the mosaic to its final location, carrying it on a board to prevent any tesserae coming loose. Cut out the tracing paper design and draw around it on the wall or floor. Spread cement-based tile adhesive over this area using a notched trowel, then press the mosaic into it, paper side up. Leave to dry for about two hours, then dampen the paper with a sponge and gently peel it away. Leave to dry overnight. Cut the tiles for the dress and the crown into quarter

10 Using cement-based tile adhesive, grout the mosaic. Clean off any excess cement with a sponge and leave the mosaic to dry overnight.

11 Remove any remaining cement with abrasive paper. Alternatively, dilute hydrochloric acid can be used, but you must wear goggles and rubber gloves and apply it outside or where there is good ventilation. Wash any acid residue from the surface with plenty of water. Finish by polishing the mosaic with a soft cloth.

CRAZY PAVING CHAIR

This chair was found rejected and battered in a junk store. With a little work and imagination, it has been transformed into an unusual, exciting piece of furniture. While mosaic may not be the first choice for covering an object such as a chair, this example shows the extremes to which the medium can successfully be taken. A whole dining suite decorated in this manner would be a major undertaking for any individual, but parts of a chair, say the seat or back-rest, could be decorated relatively easily. It is important to realise that large three-dimensional objects such as this chair, which has been covered with tesserae cut from a selection of china, require a deceptively large amount of mosaic to cover them. You would be lucky to find enough of the same pattern to cover a whole chair. Here, the problem has been solved by using slightly different patterns of china to cover different sections of the chair.

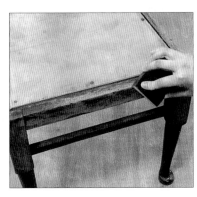

1 If the chair you have chosen has a padded seat, remove it. There may be a wooden pallet beneath the padding, which you can use as a base for the mosaic. If not, cut a piece of plywood to fit in its place.

2 Strip the chair of any paint or varnish and sand down with coarse-grade abrasive paper. Then paint the whole chair with diluted PVA glue.

3 When the surface is dry, stick the seat in place with a strong wood glue and fill any gaps around the edge with cement-based tile adhesive mixed with an admix for extra strength and flexibility.

Materials and Equipment You Will Need

Chair • 2cm (¾in) plywood sheet (optional) • Paint or varnish stripper • Coarse-grade abrasive paper • Paintbrush • PVA (white) glue • Wood glue • Cement-based tile adhesive • Admix for tile adhesive • Mixing container • Flexible knife • Pencil or chalk • Large selection of china • Tile nippers • Rubber gloves • Dilute hydrochloric acid (optional) • Goggles (optional) • Soft cloth

4 Draw a design or motifs on any large flat surfaces of the chair with a pencil or chalk. Use simple shapes that are easy to read; this chair will have a large flower on the seat and a heart on the back-rest.

5 Select china with colours and patterns to suit the motifs you have drawn. Using tile nippers, cut the china into the appropriate shapes and sizes.

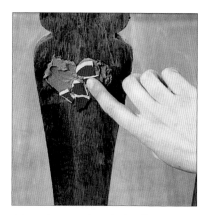

6 Spread cement-based tile adhesive, with admix, within the areas of your design and press the cut china firmly into it.

7 Select china to cover the rest of the chair. As you are unlikely to have enough of the same pattern to cover the whole chair, choose two or three patterns that look good together. Cut the china into small, varied shapes.

8 Working on small areas at a time, tile the rest of the chair as in step 6. Where one section of wood meets another, change the pattern of the china you are using.

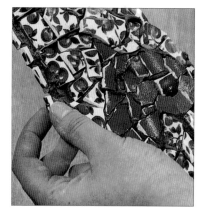

9 Cut appropriately patterned china into thin slivers and use these to tile the edges of any thin sections of wood. Here, the edges of the back-rest are covered. Leave to dry for at least 24 hours. ▶

10 Mix up some more cement-based tile adhesive with the admix. Using a flexible knife, smooth this grout into the four corners of every piece of wood. Wearing rubber gloves, rub the grout over the flat surfaces. Work on a small area at a time and try to clean off most of the excess as you go. Leave overnight to dry.

11 Sand off the excess cement. This can be quite a difficult job, as there are many awkward angles. Alternatively, dilute hydrochloric acid can be used, but you must wear goggles and rubber gloves and apply it outside or where there is good ventilation. Wash any acid residue from the surface with plenty of water and, when dry, polish with a soft cloth.

HOUSE NUMBER PLAQUE

Hung on a door frame or fence post, this striking number plaque, designed by Sarah Round, will catch the eye of passers-by. It is made with tesserae cut from brightly coloured tiles and small pieces of mirror. As this piece will be left outside all year round and will have to face all weather conditions, it may be a good idea to paint the areas of grout with a transparent water sealant. If you do this, make sure you clean any sealant from the surface of the tiles. A larger plaque could be made to display a house name.

1 Cut a piece of 1cm (½in) chipboard to size; the one used here is 18 x 15cm (7 x 6in). Draw the house number on the chipboard, making sure it is at least 1.5cm (⅝in) wide. If you wish, you can also mark the intended positions of the mirror.

2 Paint the chipboard, front, back and sides, with diluted PVA glue. Leave to dry.

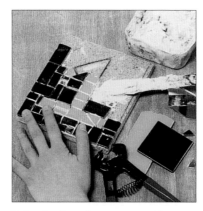

3 Cut the tiles and mirror into small pieces using tile nippers. First tile the number with the tesserae you have cut, sticking them on the base, a small area at a time, with waterproof tile adhesive. Then tile the area around the number, cutting and applying small pieces of mirror to the marked positions. Wipe off any excess tile adhesive and leave the plaque to dry for 24 hours.

4 Cover the surface with black outdoor tile grout, making sure all the gaps between the tesserae are well filled, as no moisture must be allowed to penetrate the chipboard base. Spread the grout along the edges of the plaque, then leave to dry for about 10 minutes. Wipe off the excess grout with a sponge and leave the plaque to dry for a further 24 hours. Paint the back of the plaque with an exterior paint and fix a clip for hanging. Finish by polishing the surface of the plaque with a dry soft cloth and clear glass polish.

Materials and Equipment You Will Need

1cm (½in) chipboard (particle board) • Saw • Felt-tipped pen • PVA (white) glue • Paintbrushes • Tiles in two contrasting colours • Mirror • Tile nippers • Tile adhesive • Mixing container • Flexible knife • Black ready-mixed outdoor tile grout • Grout spreader • Sponge • Waterproof exterior paint • Wall fastening • Screws • Screwdriver • Soft cloth • Clear glass polish

GARDEN URN

This unusual garden urn is decorated with modern faces but has a look that is reminiscent of Byzantine icons. Many people will shy away from attempting to draw the human form, but it is worth a try; a simple and naive drawing can look better than more realistic depictions when rendered in mosaic. Use a frost-resistant terracotta pot, and if it is not glazed you must varnish the inside to stop moisture seeping through from the inside and pushing off the tesserae. This is especially important if the urn is to be used for plants left outside. As this is one of the more ambitious projects in the book, it is best tackled after you have had a chance to experiment on smaller objects.

1 Paint the inside of the urn with yacht varnish. Leave to dry.

3 Choose a dark colour from the range of vitreous glass for the main outlines and details such as eyes and lips. Cut these into eighths using tile nippers. Mix up cement-based tile adhesive and stick the tesserae to the lines of your drawing.

5 Working on a small area at a time, apply cement-based tile adhesive to the face and press the tesserae into it. Use a mixture of all the colours, but in areas of shade use more of the darker tesserae and in highlighted areas use more of the lighter pieces. ▶

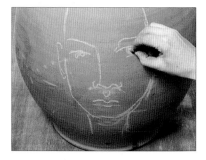

2 Divide the pot into quarters and draw your design on each quarter with chalk. The design used here depicts four different heads and shoulders. Try to keep the drawing very simple, sketching just the basic elements of the face.

4 Select a range of colours for the flesh tones and cut into quarters.

Materials and Equipment You Will Need
Large frost-resistant urn • Yacht varnish • Paintbrush • Chalk • Vitreous glass mosaic tiles • Tile nippers • Cement-based tile adhesive •
Mixing container • Flexible knife • Rubber gloves • Sponge • Abrasive paper • Dilute hydrochloric acid (optional) • Goggles (optional)

6 Choose colours for the area surrounding the heads. Spread these out on a clean table to see if they work together. A mixture of blues and whites with a little green has been chosen here. Cut the pieces into quarters.

8 Mix up more tile adhesive and, wearing rubber gloves, spread it over the surface of the mosaic. Do this very thoroughly, making sure you fill all the gaps between the tesserae. This is especially important if the urn is going to be situated outside. Wipe off any excess cement with a sponge, then leave to dry for 24 hours.

10 Finish off the urn by rubbing tile adhesive over the lip and inside the pot. This prevents the mosaic from seeming to end abruptly and gives the urn and mosaic a more unified appearance.

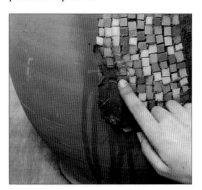

7 Working on a small area at a time, spread tile adhesive on to the surface and press the cut vitreous glass into it, making sure the colours are arranged randomly. Cover the entire outer surface of the urn with tesserae, then leave to dry for 24 hours.

9 Use abrasive paper to remove any cement that has dried on the surface of the mosaic. If the cement is proving hard to remove, dilute hydrochloric acid can be used, but you must wear goggles and rubber gloves and apply it outside or where there is good ventilation. Wash any acid residue from the surface with plenty of water. Leave to dry.

MOSAIC PANEL

This richly textured panel designed by Cleo Mussi is composed of tesserae cut from a variety of patterned china. Motifs are cut out and used as focal points for the patterns; some are raised to give them extra emphasis. These are surrounded and separated by tesserae arranged to form strong linear elements. The design has been stuck on to a plywood base, rather than directly on to the wall surface, to create a more three-dimensional effect. This also gives the panel the advantage of being portable.

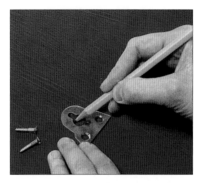

1 Draw the outer shape of the panel on to a sheet of 2cm (¾in) plywood. If you are unsure about drawing directly on to the surface, make a stencil from thick cardboard. Cut out around this shape using a jigsaw and sand down the rough edges. Seal one side and the edges with diluted PVA glue. Paint the unsealed side (the back) with wood primer, undercoat and then gloss paint, allowing each coat to dry before applying the next.

2 Mark the position of the mirror on the back of the panel. Using the appropriate drill bit, rebate (rabbet) the area that will be under the keyhole-shaped opening, large enough to take a screw head. Screw the mirror plate in position.

3 Draw your design on the sealed top surface. If necessary, trace and transfer your original design. Tools such as rulers, T squares and a pair of compasses will be helpful if your design incorporates geometric elements.

▶

Materials and Equipment You Will Need

2cm (¾in) plywood sheet • Pencil • Thick cardboard (optional) • Jigsaw (saber saw) • Abrasive paper • PVA (white) glue • Paintbrushes • Wood primer • White undercoat • Gloss paint • Mirror plate • Drill and rebate (rabbet) bit • 2 x 2cm (¾in) screws • Screwdriver • Tracing paper (optional) • Ruler, T square or pair of compasses (optional) • Selection of china • Tile nippers • Tile adhesive • Powdered tile grout • Mixing container • Cement dye, vinyl matt emulsion or acrylic paint (optional) • Rubber gloves • Squeegee or flexible knife • Nailbrush • Soft cloth

4 Sort the china into groups according to colour and pattern and select interesting motifs that could be used to form the centrepieces of designs. Using the tile nippers, cut the china pieces into the desired shapes.

5 Using smooth edges cut from cups and plates and ready-mixed tile adhesive, tile the edges of the panel. Then use small, regular-shaped tesserae to tile the structural lines of the design. Press the pieces in the adhesive first.

6 Raise small areas of the mosaic to give greater emphasis to sections of the design by setting the tesserae on a larger mound of tile adhesive. Cut more china and use it to form the patterns between the structural lines. Leave the panel to dry for 24 hours.

7 Mix powdered grout with water. If you wish the grout to have a colour, add cement dye, vinyl matt emulsion or acrylic paint to the mixture (if this is to be used indoors, cement dye is not essential). Wearing rubber gloves, spread the grout over the surface using a squeegee or a flexible knife. Rub the grout into the gaps with your fingers.

8 Allow the surface to dry for a few minutes, then scrub off any excess grout using a stiff nailbrush.

9 Leave to dry for 24 hours, then polish the surface with a soft cloth.

TEMPLATES

PRINCESS WALL MOSAIC p.79–81

BATHROOM CABINET p.46–7

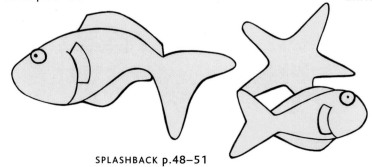

SPLASHBACK p.48–51

SUPPLIERS

The majority of the materials needed to make these mosaic projects can be found in most DIY or hardware stores. Most large tile stores will order specialist mosaic materials for you if they do not have them in stock. Listed below are some of the better known specialist suppliers, as well as suppliers used by the artists when making the projects illustrated in this book.

SUPPLIERS

UK
Edgar Udney and Co Ltd
314 Balham High Road
London SW17
Tel: 020 8767 818

Felicity Evans
'Six Smiths'
Arch 11, Culvert Place
London SW11 5BA
Tel: 020 7498 2977

Langley London Ltd
The Tile Centre
161–167 Borough High Street
London SE1 1HU
Tel: 020 7407 4444

Mosaic Trader UK
www.mosaictraderuk.com

Paul Fricker Ltd
452 Pinhoe Road
Exeter
Devon EX4 8HN
Tel: 01392 468 440

Reed Harris Ltd
Riverside House
Carnworth Road
London SW6 3HS
Tel: 020 7736 7511
www.reedharris.co.uk/

Tower Ceramics
89–95 Parkway
Camden Town
London NW1 7PP
Tel: 020 7485 7192
www.towerceramics.co.uk/

World's End Tiles
Silverthorne Road

Battersea
London SW8 3HE
Tel: 020 7819 2100
www.worldsendtiles.co.uk/

USA
Mosaic Trader
Tel: 1-954-638-4360
www.mosaictraderusa.com/

Witsend Mosaic
Tel: 1-888-494-8736 or (920) 822-7666
http://www.witsendmosaic.com

Italy
Lucio Orsoni
Cannaregio 1045
30121 Venezia
Italy
Tel: 041 717255
www.orsoni.com/

Australia
Camden Arts Centre Pty Ltd
188–200 Gertrude Street
Fitzroy
Victoria
Australia 3065

WM Crosbey (Merchandise) Pty Ltd
266-274 King Street
Melbourne
Australia 3000

Rodda Pty Ltd
62 Beach Street
Port Melbourne
Victoria
Australia

See http://mosaicmatters.co.uk/ for a list of mosaic suppliers in 17 countries worldwide

ACKNOWLEDGEMENTS

The author would like to thank Bill and Theresa Baird for all their help during the course of making this book.

The author and publishers would also like to thank the following for their contributions: Tessa Brown, Sandra Hadfield, Cleo Mussi, Sarah Round and Norma Vondee.

Thanks also to Gideon at Upstart Gallery, and all the mosaicists who lent their pieces for photography.

INDEX